Mammals

Mammals

By Jaromír Zpěvák

SUNBURST BOOKS

Text by Jaromír Zpěvák
Translated by Marie Carrollová
Illustrations by Jaromír Zpěvák
Graphic design by Ivan Zpěvák

Designed and produced by Aventinum
English language edition first published in 1994
by Sunburst Books, Deacon House,
65 Old Church Street, London SW3 5BS

ISBN 1 85778 033 7
Printed in Slovakia
1/25/02/51-01

CONTENTS

INTRODUCTION

The first mammals appeared on the Earth as early as the Mesozoic era, at the end of the Triassic period, about 200 million years ago. In those days, the world was ruled by highly developed reptilians. Apart from the huge dinosaurs — giant lizards — there were smaller, even tiny, ones. These inconspicuous 'lizards' underwent great evolutionary changes. The position and angle of their limbs shifted, different sorts of teeth developed, fur replaced scales and sweat glands changed into milk glands. The first, primitive mammals were hardly as big as a rabbit and they looked a little like modern insect-eating mammals, such as moles. However, they already had a stable body temperature and quite a large brain that was capable of further development.

One hundred million years ago our planet experienced enormous volcanic activity. The crust of the Earth moved and the climate changed abruptly. The old Mesozoic world was fading away. Most of the lizards could not cope with the new conditions. Dinosaurs, pterosaurs — the flying lizards — and a lot of species of sea creatures died out. The mammals had lost their enemies and so started to multiply very fast. They were able to adapt to the new conditions and soon took over all suitable places on the land and in the water. Eventually, species that could fly like birds developed. The first mammals were omnivorous, that is, they ate both plant and animal food. Later, they became either herbivorous — plant-eating — or carnivorous — meat-eating. Just as the Mesozoic era was the period of dinosaurs, the Tertiary or Cenozoic era belonged to mammals. Ancient species perished and new ones developed. At the end of this period, some two million years ago, humans appeared on the Earth.

How do we know all these facts? Imprints of plants and animals' bodies, receptacles, fossilized carapaces, shells and bones were preserved in the sediment of shallow seas, lakes and swamps, under sand drifts and in peat bogs, caves and volcanic ash. Scientists collect these remains, analyse and classify them. They can tell quite accurately what a certain animal looked like, where and how it lived and what enemies it had. In addition, engravings, paintings and sculptures made by primitive people about 30,000 years ago show the animals they hunted and, later, the domesticated animals of the last Ice Age. The discovery of these pictures and models was very important for scientific knowledge.

To begin with, people ate seeds, fruits and edible bulbs, but they soon learned how to make tools and weapons. They mastered fire and became hunters. In time, they domesticated some animals and travelled across the land with their grazing herds. Eventually, people settled down in one place and began to grow plants. Forests gave way to fields and the first settlements appeared; later towns were founded. Humans were changing nature — they irrigated dry areas, dried out swamps and exploited minerals. They completely destroyed some species of animals and brought others to live in places, where they had never lived before — unfortunately, this was usually to the detriment of nature.

In the 19th and 20th centuries, industry, transport and construction developed so fast that living conditions deteriorated rapidly. Many species of plants and animals died out and many others are still threatened with extinction. People started to realize that they must protect nature, not only by creating conservation areas such as national parks, but also by careful treatment of waste water, prevention of air pollution and limitation of the use of poisons and chemicals in agriculture, forestry and other areas of land management. There is no other option — for if nature dies, the human race will die with it.

WHAT IS A MAMMAL?

A mammal is a creature whose first food is its mother's milk.

Teats supplying the milk are usually arranged in two rows under the animal's chest and belly.

In some mammals, there is only one pair on the chest

or in the groins.

In hoofed animals, called ungulates, two or four nipples form a special organ — the udder.

WHAT THE TEETH TELL US

Teeth are divided into four types, according to their purpose in coping with food. These are incisors, canines, premolars and molars. In primitive species, the teeth cannot be differentiated; some of them have none.

The Platypus does not need teeth. Although its jaws are far more sensitive than a duck's bill, they can break the shells of water creatures. To chew, its lower jaw moves from side to side.

The Anteater also has no teeth. Its jaws are joined together to form a narrow tube. It has a sticky tongue 50 cm long that it can slide out of this tube. Its muscular stomach grinds its food — ants and termites that it catches on its sticky tongue.

The Mole feeds mainly on insects. All its teeth are sharply pointed.

The Bat eats insects, too. Therefore, its incisors and molars are sharp. The individual types of teeth are already quite well distinctive.

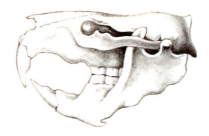

The Beaver is a typical rodent. Its long, chisel-shaped incisors are covered with tooth enamel only on the front. The backs of the teeth are continuously rubbed away so that they always have sharp edges. They grow during the whole of the beaver's life. The canines are absent and the premolars and molars have bulges for grinding hard plant food.

The Hare's teeth are similar to those of rodents, but behind the upper pair of large incisors, there is a second, shorter and pointed pair. The enamel covers their whole surface.

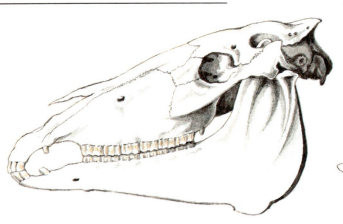

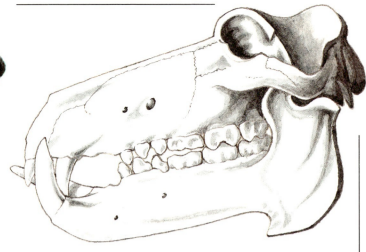

The Horse's slanting incisors are rubbed away when plucking grass. We can tell a horse's age by the condition of these teeth. A horse's premolars and molars have bands of hard enamel. Only adult horses have canine teeth.

The Hippopotamus has 40 teeth. The incisors are long and the lower canines form tusks which are 50 cm long. The upper canines are shorter, three-sided and blunt at the end like a pig's.

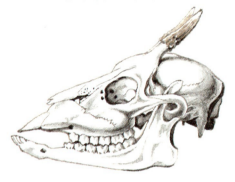

The Roe Deer plucks grass with its lower jaw and upper lip. Huntsmen can judge the animal's age from the extent to which the premolars and molars of the right side of the lower jaw have worn down.

The Musk-deer's teeth are similar, but the upper canines stick out 10 cm from its muzzle. They are used for searching for food under the snow and for duelling for females, as the musk deer has no antlers.

The Elephant's upper canines grow into giant tusks. They are not covered with enamel and they grow throughout the animal's life. They are used for digging out roots and bulbs, but never as weapons. Canines, premolars and lower incisors are absent. Worn molars are replaced with new ones which grow gradually. That happens about six times during the animal's life. There are strips of hard enamel on the grinding surface of the molars.

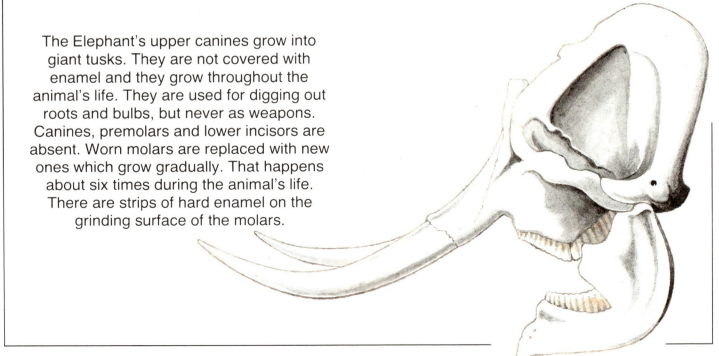

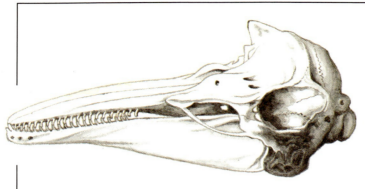

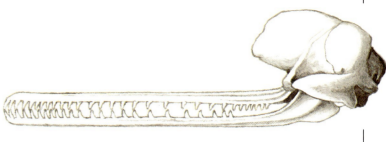

The Susu eats fish and, therefore, its pointed teeth are all the same shape.

The Porpoise feeds mainly on fish. It has approximately one hundred conical teeth which do not differ in shape.

The Seal has similar teeth, but no tusks. It gulps fish in big pieces, so it swallows small stones to mash the food in its stomach.

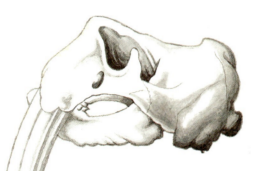

The Walrus's incisors, canines and even its molars have sharp points. The upper canines extend into strong tusks, helping the animal to tear molluscs and crustaceans from the sea bed and to climb ice floes.

The Whale feeds on plankton, tiny floating sea creatures and plants. It swims with its mouth open and lets the water, which is filled with tiny sea animals, flow into it. Instead of teeth, its upper jaw is equipped with pairs of elastic fringed whalebones, through which it sieves its catch with its tongue.

The Cat has typical meat-eating teeth — small but sharp incisors, big and slightly curved canines and premolars and molars with sharp edges. The strongest last upper premolar and the first lower molar are the so-called laniary, or tearing teeth.

The Wolf's canines are robust and its laniary teeth are very well developed. It also has premolars and molars.

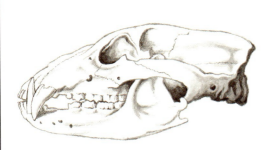

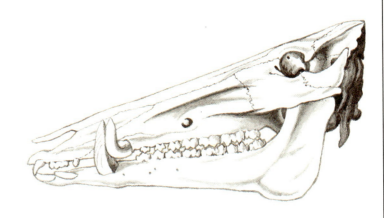

The Brown Bear eats meat and also plants, so it is omnivorous. Its laniary teeth, therefore, are not so clearly distinguished.

The Wild Boar is also omnivorous. It uses its tusks for tearing roots and for defence. Its lower sharp canine is called a rip tooth.

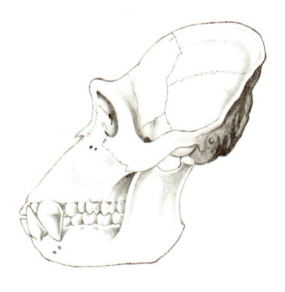

The Ring-tailed Lemur, prosimian, eats mixed food. It has 36 teeth.

The Gorilla is an anthropoid and has 32 teeth, the same number as humans.

THE PURPOSE OF HIND LEGS

Mammals' legs are adapted to the environment and conditions in which they live. Some walk on the whole sole of the foot and all the toes; others only walk on certain toes, while the other toes are not developed or may even be absent. This is best seen on the skeleton. The general rule is that the longer the legs and the less contact with the ground, the faster the animal moves.

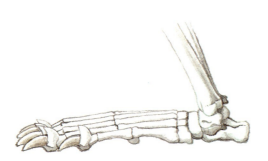

The Bear uses the whole sole of the foot. It is called a plantigrade animal — a 'flat-sole-walker'.

The Dog walks on four toes. The bones of its toes are cushioned with pads. It is a digitigrade animal — 'toe-walker'.

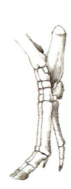

The Rhinoceros has only three developed toes — the second, third and fourth.

The Pig has only two fully developed toes. The second and the fifth are shorter; they are called 'false hooves' and prevent the animal from sinking into muddy ground.

The Horse is the best long-distance runner. It only treads on one toe — the third toe — which touches the ground with just the protruding edge of the hoof.

The ends of the toes were originally provided with claws. In some groups of mammals, they changed subsequently into flat nails; in others they changed into hooves.

Wolf

Rhesus Monkey

Cattle

HOW MAMMALS USE THEIR FORELEGS

The front limbs are sometimes used for special work. Therefore, they are different from the hind limbs.

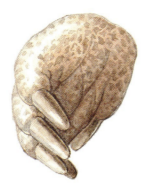

The Mole's front legs are short, broad and equipped with flat claws. When the mole digs, they work as a shovel.

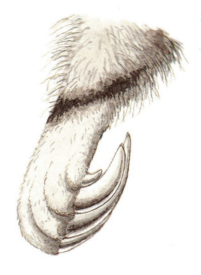

The Anteater rakes up the nests of termites, which are as hard as concrete. It supports itself on its toe joints to protect its big, strong and sharp claws.

The Bat flies. It does not have true wings, but a sensitive flying membrane stretched between its prolonged toes, forearms, the body and hind legs. The short toe provided with a claw is used for cleaning its fur.

The Sea Lion is a sea animal, which sometimes climbs ashore. Its legs have developed to a perfect oar shape.

The Koala is good at climbing smooth branches. It is able to grip by using its 'hands' which have two fingers in the opposite direction to the other three. Only the thumb does not have long sharp claws.

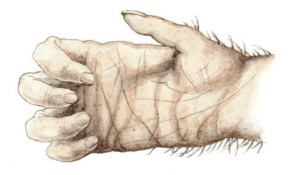

The Chimpanzee's thumb moves in a different way to the rest of the fingers forming a real hand, which can function nearly as well as a human hand.

WHAT THE SURFACE OF THE BODY TELLS US

Mammals have a constant temperature. Fur or hair helps to keep it stable. Fur or hair has the same origin as birds' feathers and reptiles' scales. It may range from a soft, warm, silky coat to coarse, long bristles. Fur is renewed in the spring and in the autumn. Summer fur is usually thinner and shorter; winter fur is thicker and longer. The body surface may also be covered with prickles, horny plates, scales, or it can be completely bare.

The Horse, as a prairie animal, has short and dense hair.

The Water Shrew needs especially thick fur to prevent water from penetrating to the body.

The Musk-ox spends all its time in snow and ice, so its long and thick fur is the warmest of all.

The Bactrian Camel lives in rough mountain conditions and often has to lie in the snow. Long woollen hair on the lower part of the body protects it in the winter.

The Hare has so-called loose fur, which sheds easily. An enemy, trying to catch it, is often left with only a bunch of fur in its mouth.

The Wild Boar is covered with rough bristles.

The Armadillo, confronted by an enemy, rolls up into a small ball. Its head and back are protected by horny plates; thick bristles grow through their joins and on its belly.

The Pangolin looks like a big fir cone. Its body is covered with hard horny scales.

The Hedgehog has sharp prickles on its neck and back. Special muscles help it to roll up into a prickly ball when it is in danger.

The Porcupine is armed with long and strong prickles, which it can 'shoot' over several metres.

The Elephant is born sparsely covered with hair which it loses when it grows up. A tassel of strong hair remains at the end of the tail.

The Dolphin never leaves the water. Its skin is completely naked and smooth. It is protected against the cold by a layer of fat.

HOW WE CLASSIFY MAMMALS

Mammals are classified according to the development of their embryos — babies before they are born — and according to specific significant characteristics of their body structure.

EGG-LAYING MAMMALS

VIVIPAROUS MAMMALS
       P O U C H E D M A M M A L S

       P L A C E N T A L M A M M A L S
         INSECTIVORES

       FLYING MAMMALS

       PRIMATES
         PROSIMIANS

        MONKEYS

     E D E N T A T E S
       SLOTHS

       ANTEATERS

       ARMADILLOS

PHOLIDOTA

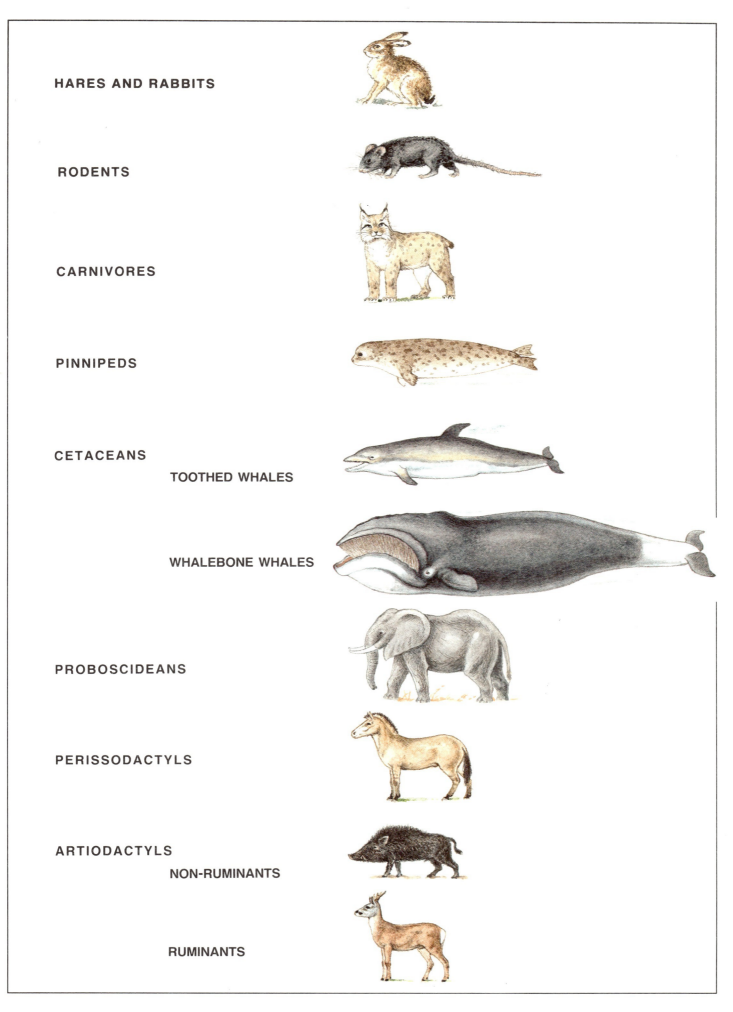

HARES AND RABBITS

RODENTS

CARNIVORES

PINNIPEDS

CETACEANS

        TOOTHED WHALES

        WHALEBONE WHALES

PROBOSCIDEANS

PERISSODACTYLS

ARTIODACTYLS

        NON-RUMINANTS

        RUMINANTS

THE BEST-KNOWN MAMMALS

EGG-LAYING MAMMALS

These sorts of mammals lay eggs with leathery shells similar to their ancestors — reptiles. They suckle their young with thick milk that oozes from a small area on the mother's abdomen, which the young lick off. Like birds, egg-laying mammals still have a third, transparent eyelid, called the nictitating membrane. They live secluded in Australia and Tasmania.

The **Australian Echidna** is a nocturnal animal — that is, it is active at night. Therefore, it has highly developed senses of smell and hearing. Its back hairs have changed to spines. The tongue can slide out from its tender, tube-like snout; with its sticky saliva it is used for hunting ants and termites. It uses its strong, sharp claws for tearing hard termite nests and for burrowing rapidly into the ground to protect itself from predators. When in danger, it rolls into a ball like a hedgehog. At the end of the summer, the female lays a single egg, which she carries in a pouch on her abdomen. As a result of the temperature of the mother's body, a tiny young animal hatches quite early and grows very fast.

The **Platypus**, an inhabitant of quiet, overgrown rivers, is very rare and strictly protected. It has greasy fur. Its wide snout looks like a duck's bill. It searches in muddy water for insects, worms and slugs. In the river banks it digs burrows several metres long, with entrances under the water, and strews the den with water plants. The female lays up to three eggs. She curls round them to incubate them. Once hatched, the young grow very slowly.

VIVIPAROUS MAMMALS

These mammals give birth to live young, which is more convenient and secure than laying eggs. Therefore, they are positioned higher on the evolutionary ladder.

POUCHED MAMMALS

There are 250 species of pouched mammals, mainly in Australia. They are herbivorous (plant-eating), insectivorous (insect-eating) as well as carnivorous (meat-eating). Their young are born as simple embryos and finish their development outside their mothers' bodies. The females of most of the species have a skin pouch around milk teats supported by special bones.

The **Grey Kangaroo** grows to the height of an adult man. It eats grass and the leaves of bushes. At any sign of danger, the whole herd, led by a mature male, rushes, panic-stricken to escape. The Grey Kangaroo is an excellent runner. It can cover as much as 10 metres in one leap. In the bush it can hardly be beaten, even by a fast horse.

The **Koala** feeds exclusively on the leaves of the eucalyptus tree. It only climbs down to the ground only to reach another tree. The mother carries her growing young on her back.

PLACENTAL MAMMALS

These mammals give birth to more developed young than the pouched mammals because the embryo stays longer in the mother's body. It is nourished through its mother's placenta.

INSECTIVORES

These represent the most ancient order of higher mammals. They live all over the world apart from Australia and South America. They are usually small animals and need a proportionately huge amount of food. They feed mostly on insects, but they must also have meat and herbs. They walk on the whole sole of the foot.

The **European Hedgehog** goes hunting at twilight; it snorts and stamps very loudly. It catches insects, slugs, lizards and snakes, but also likes eggs, fruit, acorns and beech nuts. It is highly resistant to poisons. If a viper bites its unprotected snout, it takes several hours for a hedgehog to die. There are two species: the Western Hedgehog, living in north-west Europe, and the Eastern Hedgehog, living in south-east Europe.

The **Common Mole** digs a network of underground passages and checks them several times a day, searching for earthworms, grubs and insects. It catches frogs, lizards or mice. It hoards reserves for times of need. It paralyzes earthworms by biting their nerve centres, so that they stay alive, but cannot escape. It builds its nest away from its hunting grounds and surrounds it with a ring of passages with many exits. There are a lot of parasites in its nest, especially mole fleas. The mole moves very fast on the ground and, in danger, it will even swim across a river.

The **Common Shrew**, the most frequently encountered species of shrew, is active during the whole year. It is easily distinguished from the mouse by its long muscular snout, which is always in motion. In darkness — like bats — it emits a very high-frequency sound, which we cannot hear, and it gets its bearings from the echo. Besides insects and worms, it also hunts frogs and small birds. It will also scavenge dead animals. It gives birth to as many as ten young, but it also has a lot of enemies.

FLYING MAMMALS

There are thousands of species of flying mammals, mainly in the tropics and subtropics. They are nocturnal animals, that is, they are active at night. With the exception of the Malayan Fruit Bats, they emit sounds which are so highly pitched that the human ear cannot hear them. The echo is detected by the bats' very sensitive hearing, so that they can avoid all obstacles during their flight and even catch flying insects.

The **Malayan Fruit Bat** lives in the islands of Malaysia. Its wing-span may be as great as 1.5 metres. It has quite big eyes. By eating fruit it creates a lot of damage in orchards. People hunt it and its meat is considered a delicacy.

The **Common Vampire Bat** is one of the few species that feeds on blood. During the night it attacks cattle in pastures. It cuts a small hole in the animal's skin with its sharp teeth and consumes the blood. This results in the transmission of various infectious diseases, particularly rabies. It lives only in tropical Africa.

The **Lesser Horseshoe Bat**, with membraneous growths on its snout, is becoming increasingly rare. It sleeps during the day in attics, cellars or caves, often in large flocks. It sleeps hanging upside-down.

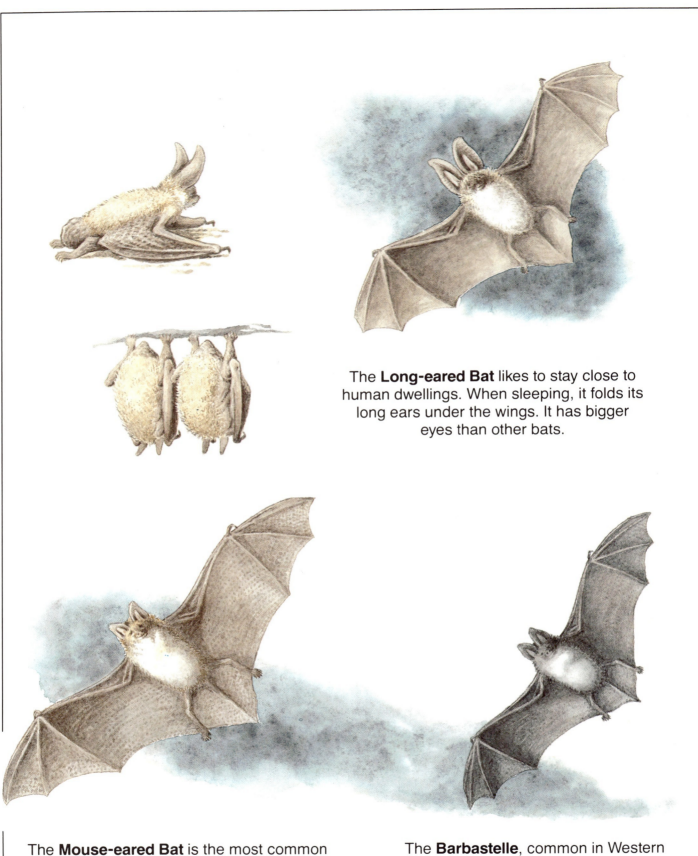

The **Long-eared Bat** likes to stay close to human dwellings. When sleeping, it folds its long ears under the wings. It has bigger eyes than other bats.

The **Mouse-eared Bat** is the most common bat species. It flies in straight lines. During the summer the males stay apart from the females who care for the young. They travel some 250 km to their winter habitat, where they sleep in huge flocks, crowded close to one another.

The **Barbastelle**, common in Western Europe, prefers wooded country. It catches small insects.

PRIMATES

Primates spend most of their lives in the tops of trees. They usually have five fingers and can use the thumb in opposition to the other fingers. As their eyes are positioned in front, they have perfect vision. Normally only one young animal is born at a time. It can see immediately, but is dependent on its mother's care for a long time. The first milk teeth are replaced by permanent teeth later on. They feed on insects, small vertebrates, eggs and fruit.

PROSIMIANS

These are lower primates. As nocturnal animals, they have excellent senses of smell and sight. They will not fall from a tree, even when sleeping. If they bend their limbs, the fingers grasp automatically. They carry their young across the abdomen in a skin fold. Two-thirds of all prosimians live in the primeval forests of Madagascar, the rest live in Africa, India and Malaysia.

The **Ring-tailed Lemur**, with its long, striped tail, is often seen in zoos. It likes to expose its belly to the sun's rays.

The **Philippine Tarsier** has long insteps on its hind legs and adhesive discs rather like a tree-frog. It is able to jump as far as a metre through the trees. It lives in permanent couples in south-east Asia. The female carries her young in her mouth, in the same way as the insect-eating mammals.

MONKEYS

These animals are active in the daytime. The soles of their feet and the palms of their hands are hairless. The claws of most monkeys have changed into flat nails. On the ground they move on all fours, only exceptionally standing on their hind legs. They are wasteful with food, destroying more than they eat.

FLAT-NOSED MONKEYS

These are called New-World Monkeys, since they live in South and Central America. They have a wide nose partition, and their nostrils open to the sides. A number of species have sensitive, prehensile tails. They carry their young on the backs. Their biggest enemy is the harpy eagle.

The **Brown Capuchin** is a favourite in the zoos. When climbing trees, it winds its long tail around the branches; while on the ground, it holds it rolled up. It is a clever and skilled monkey and uses stones for breaking nutshells.

The **Red Howler Monkey** defends its territory with loud shrieks. It lives in small groups in the forests of the Amazon and never climbs down from the tree to the ground. Its prehensile tail is the most well-developed of all the monkeys. It feeds on leaves and fruit.

NARROW-NOSED MONKEYS

These are also called Old-World Monkeys because they live in Europe, Asia and Africa. They have a narrow nasal partition and their nostrils open downwards. With their hairless faces, the number of teeth and the shape of their ears they are similar to people. Narrow-nosed monkeys live in groups. Every group is led by a mature male, who is obeyed by everyone without resistance. Monkeys like to stroke each other's fur, although they never have fleas. They enjoy eating the salty skin scales — the dandruff. Social grooming improves their relationships. Narrow-nosed monkeys carry their young on their abdomens.

The **Green Monkey**, a colourful and beautiful monkey, with a round head, uses its long tail as a rudder when it jumps. It lives in damp forests and stays close to villages. It consumes huge quantities of corn, plant sprouts and fruit, but it wastes even more food. Its range extends from Senegal and Ethiopia to south Africa.

The **Mantled Baboon** moves on the ground, where it looks for bulbs and tubers, and small animals under stones. It is a strong monkey with ferocious teeth. It can throw stones. Not even a leopard has the courage to attack a group of baboons.

APES

The apes are the biggest primates. They have no tails and can live up to 50 years. The development of the young in the female's abdomen takes nine months, and its upbringing several years. Apes live in the trees and they are insecure on the ground. They have the most developed brain of all animals. They are prone to human diseases like flu and tuberculosis. They are extremely afraid of snakes and cannot swim.

The **Orang-utan**, 'the forest man', of Borneo and Sumatra, has extremely long arms and its head is wedged between the shoulders. The males have cheek pouches which help them create a sound that penetrates the wide silence of the forest. The females wander alone with their young, which only mature after eight to ten years. Orang-utans are in danger of extinction.

The **Chimpanzee** lives in the equatorial forests of Africa. Sometimes it enjoys eating antelope meat or the young of monkeys. It moves on the ground always close to the trees. It loves rhythm; it jumps, stamps, claps its hands and, sometimes, it even drums on hollow stems. It marks its territory with loud yelling. It can be very cunning, when trying to reach some delicacy.

The **Gorilla** can grow to 1.8 metres in height and over 250 kg in weight. It has enormous strength. Therefore, it has no natural enemies except people. It lives in equatorial Africa and is completely herbivorous. The females sleep with their young in nests in trees, while the males stay on the ground. There are very few gorillas and they are strictly protected.

EDENTATES

These small animals differ widely in appearance. They are the survivors of a big order which thrived in the Tertiary age. They depend on their sense of smell. Their young are born quite mature.

The **Two-toed Sloth** spends its entire life in the trees, hanging by its four legs, which have strong claws. As it hangs upside-down, its hair grows in a different direction — from the soles of its feet to the shoulders and from the abdomen to its back — so that rain will run off easily. Green algae grow in its fur so that it can hide in the green leaves very well. This nocturnal creature is completely powerless on the ground. It lives in the forests of Brazil and Guyana. Its biggest enemy is the harpy eagle.

The **Anteater** lives in the vast pampas of Argentina, Paraguay and Guatemala. With its big claws, it rakes up termite and ant hills, and picks up the insects on its long tongue. It can close its nostrils, protect its eyes with heavy eyelids and the termites are not able to penetrate its thick fur. In spite of that, it takes a bath after each hunt. At night, it rolls up into a ball and covers itself with its tail. The female carries her young on her back for a whole year.

The **Armadillo** digs long warrens deep under the ground. Its burrow has up to 12 exits. It wanders through the night searching for insects, small vertebrates and sweet fruit. Its arched armour is made from individual bony strips covered with horn. It is frequently kept in zoos.

HARES AND RABBITS

The forelegs of hares and rabbits are shorter than their hind legs. They do not walk, but run or jump. When chewing, they move their lower jaws from left to right. Their dung is either the well-known droppings or, sometimes, a thin mess consisting of partially digested parts of plants. Hares eat this mess and so make complete use of this food, which is otherwise difficult to digest. As they eat not only their own dung, but also that of any hare, infectious diseases can spread very fast.

The **European Hare** only feeds at dusk. It never drinks; the water in its food is sufficient. It lives mostly in lush lowlands. It never runs straight to its 'form' — shallow nest — but jumps away in the opposite direction several times and returns following its own trail to confuse its enemies. It can see an enemy from its form much sooner than the enemy can see it, but it only starts its escape at the very last minute. During the winter, it gnaws at the bark of young trees. February is the time of mating. The female usually tries to defend herself with 'boxing' and kicking, and the hairs fly around. The first young — leverets — usually appear in March. Modern large-scale agricultural production is reducing the number of hares.

The **European Wild Rabbit** is smaller than the hare. It has shorter legs and ears and lives in colonies. It digs out underground warrens, but the female only makes a shallow burrow for the young, strewing it with her hairs. Whenever it leaves the den, it covers its exit with earth. The rabbit needs a dry, warm environment. Several domestic types of rabbit have been bred from the wild rabbit.

RODENTS

Rodents feed mainly on plant food. They have lots of young and, in favourable conditions, they breed several times a year.

The **Red Squirrel**, 'the monkey of European forests', undertakes expeditions quite far from the forest. It collects fruits, seeds and mushrooms, but also likes to nibble at the sprouts of spruces and firs and it even eats birds' young. It loves nuts, which it buries in the ground and keeps in reserve. In spite of their year-round protection, the number of squirrels has been decreasing.

The **European Suslik** lives in colonies in warm lowlands; it cannot tolerate cold and damp. It feeds on grass seeds and grain. It digs two kinds of burrows. One sort is deep and this is where it brings up its young and hibernates; the other is a shallow hiding place in the area, where it has a lot of food. The suslik's feasting places in the fields are indicated by piles of empty grain ears. Insects or mice improve the menu. The suslik does not make reserves; the whole winter it lives on the thick layer of the fat under the skin. Once a year, it gives birth to about eight young.

The **Alpine Marmot** also digs out two types of burrows — one deep and wide for the winter and one short and shallow for the summer. They live in pairs in high mountains above the forest boundary. The Alpine Marmot has excellent sight and hearing. It can spot danger from far away and signals it with a penetrating whistle.

The **European Beaver** gnaws willows, alders, aspens and other trees with its strong incisors until they eventually fall down. It eats the bark and uses the bare branches to build a 'lodge' — a big heap in the middle of stagnant water. The entrances are below water level and the den is above it. When the water level drops, the beaver builds a very strong dam downstream, even in a heavy current. It also uses clay, reeds and stones for its construction. It keeps food reserves at the lodge, so it is important that the water does not freeze down to the bottom. Hunted for its thick and beautiful fur, the beaver became extinct in Europe by the 17th century. Now, it lives mainly in Russia.

The **Fat Dormouse** begins to be active at dusk. It eats fruit, shoots and, sometimes, insects. It likes sweet fruit best. It builds its nest in hollow trees or branches. It bears up to seven young. It is a bad-tempered and snappy animal.

The **Common Dormouse** is a very peaceful little animal. It builds its round nest close to the ground or in the grass. Young are born twice a year. The winter nest is hidden under leaves between tree roots.

The **Harvest Mouse** is Europe's smallest rodent, living in reeds or cornfields. It is an excellent climber, using its tail. It feeds on grass seeds and insects.

The **Common Hamster** is a bad-tempered loner, which not only furiously defends itself, but is also aggressive. It lives in lowlands, where it digs burrows up to 2 metres deep. It feeds on corn, clover, peas, potatoes, fruit, insects and even small vertebrates. The male stores large reserves for the winter — up to 15 kg. It carries the food to the den in its cheek pouches. The female who takes care of the offspring does not have much time for making reserves, so she often starves at the end of winter.

The **Wood Mouse** has big eyes and long hind legs. It jumps and climbs very well. It lives in the undergrowth along roads and streams. In the winter it takes up residence in human houses. It searches for earthworms, insects and slugs and gathers reserves of seeds and grain. Young can be born up to three times a year. Its range extends from lowlands to mountains.

The **House Mouse** has spread across the whole world accompanying human activity, and is considered a pest by man. It gives birth to eight young several times a year, even during the winter. It can bite through walls, eating and destroying everything it comes across. In south-east Europe, the House Mouse lives in the open air, but during winter it moves into buildings.

The **Norwegian Rat** actually comes from East Asia. Travelling in the cargo holds of the ships, it has spread to all continents. It has an enormous capacity for reproduction. It does not only create damage by destroying stocks of all kind, but also by transmitting infectious diseases — even the plague. Originally, it lived in moorlands, but it is now at home in sewers and drains. It lives in groups; the bigger the group, the bolder the rats. It attacks poultry and rabbits; a large group can even attack a small child or an ill person. The human race wages a constant and inexorable war against the Norwegian Rat.

The **Black Rat**, on the contrary, likes dry places and prefers wooden buildings. It has bigger ears and a tail than the Norwegian Rat. Its fur is often black. It likes fruit. At the end of the 18th century, the much stronger and more aggressive Norwegian Rat began to drive it out of Europe.

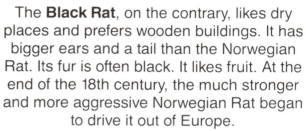

The **Water Vole** lives beside streams. It is a good swimmer. It builds a warren of burrows or makes a round nest between the roots of trees. It has up to four litters of young in a year. It stores undergound reserves of bulbs and grass. During the autumn it looks for vegetables and potatoes, in winter it gnaws at tree roots. Sometimes, it goes so far that the tree withers and dies.

The **Common Vole** differs from the mouse by having smaller eyes and ears and a shorter, hairy tail. The female can produce a litter of up to 18 young every three weeks. Therefore, Common Voles become too numerous every fourth year. While young males leave the nest, young females stay with their mother, bringing up the next generation of offspring together. The Common Vole retreats to the fields of alfalfa or clover, as they are not ploughed so often. It is our greatest trouble-maker — one vole consumes about 2 kg of grain a year. However, it has a lot of natural enemies — vultures, owls, weasels, foxes and cats.

The **Muskrat** from North America feeds mainly on water plants; sometimes it supplements its menu with molluscs or other animals. In winter, it searches for food under the ice. It builds a similar dwelling to the beaver's. Its fur is called musquash.

The **Nutria** lives in Central and South America. It was in danger of extinction, as it was hunted for its valuable fur. At present, it is a strictly protected animal. Numerous fur farms were set up all over Europe for artificial breeding.

The **Common Porcupine** is a rarity in south Europe; it lives mainly in north Africa. It wanders at night through dry lowland looking for herbs, roots and fruit. When confronted by an enemy, it either burrows into the ground or tries to frighten it away by stamping and rattling its spines. It gives birth to four young, which at birth can see and have thin spines.

The **Wild Guinea Pig** or **Cobaya** is hunted by the Indians of the Peruvian mountains for its delicious meat, which tastes like rabbit. In Europe Guinea Pigs are bred for laboratory experiments or as children's pets.

CARNIVORES

Carnivores have an excellent sense of smell and hearing and the cats have particularly good sight. All of them have well-developed scent glands and mark their hunting territory with their secretion.

The **Lion** was eradicated in south-east Europe a long time ago. It lives in the bush of Africa and about 200 animals live in the Ghir Forest in India. It hunts antelope and zebra, but is content to find a carcass. In contrast to other big cats, lions live in large groups, hunting and bringing up the young together.

The **Siberian Tiger**, the biggest and strongest living cat, is threatened with extinction in its homeland in Primorsky Kray (Russia) and Manchuria (China). Its prey consists of wild pig, deer and roebuck. It can devour up to 30 kg of flesh at once, but can subsist on mice, insects and fruit if necessary in lean times. It is svelte and can squeeze through bushes easily. Its striped fur allows it to creep close to its victims. It likes bathing and can swim across wide rivers. The female usually gives birth to four blind young. Their upbringing takes three to four years.

The **Leopard** is the most widespread of the big cats. It lives throughout Africa and the warm parts of Asia. There are many varieties, which can be identified by their size and colour. The melanic or black species is quite common — the so-called Black Panther. Leopards are extremely lithe and fast on the ground and even in the treetops. With its capacity for long jumps, it attacks antelopes and other animals; its favourite prey are monkeys, especially baboons. It usually takes its catch up a tree to devour it.

The **Jaguar** or **American Tiger** is often mistaken for the leopard, as it is very similar to the leopard both in colour and in size. It inhabits Central and South America. It lies in wait for capybara and tapir and also attacks large domestic animals. It likes water; it often bathes and can swim across wide rivers.

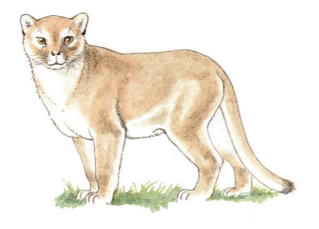

The **Mountain Lion** or **Puma** is also called the Silver Lion. It has spread, in many variations, all over the American continent from Canada to Patagonia. The biggest animals live in the north and have magnificent silver fur. The cougar can easily be tamed. If tamed from very young, it becomes devoted to its master.

The **European Wild Cat** lives all over Southern and Central Europe. It is stronger and has shorter and thicker hair on its tail than the domestic cat. It inhabits deep forests with thick undergrowth. It makes its lair in lonely warrens under fallen or hollow trees. If in danger, it carries its kittens to other hide-outs, protecting them courageously from their enemies. It catches mice, voles, birds and lizards. It can be crossbred with the domestic cat.

The **Jungle Cat** or **Caracal** lives on thick, overgrown river-banks. It is not afraid of water and is an excellent swimmer. It lies in wait, in clumps of reeds, for water birds, which it normally eats. It is found in the Nile river basin, in Asia Minor and Indonesia.

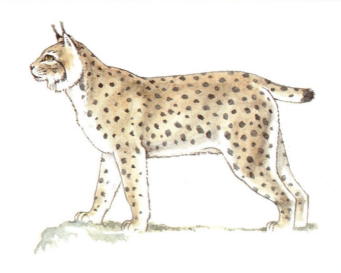

The **Lynx** moves very quietly. Like other cats, it has retractile claws. It hunts roebuck, attacking weak or sick individuals. It lies in wait for them, crouched on a tree stump or stone. It lives in Scandinavia, Eastern Europe, Asia and North America.

The **Serval** can jump to a considerable height with its long legs. It hunts smaller vertebrates, especially birds, in the African steppes. It crawls up to them in the long grass and, when they take off, it jumps and pulls them to the ground.

The **Cheetah** is an exception among the cats — it does not have retractile claws. Its long legs and the way it behaves are similar to the dog. It is an excellent runner. Over a short distance, it can run at a speed of up to 120 km per hour. When it crawls near its preys, it rushes at them. It was trained in ancient India to hunt antelopes and zebras. It inhabits steppes and forest-steppes in Asia and Africa.

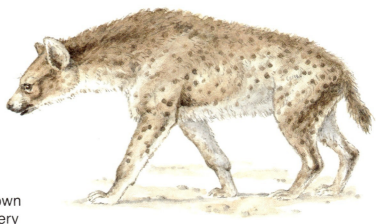

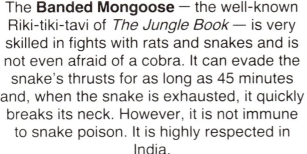

The **Banded Mongoose** — the well-known Riki-tiki-tavi of *The Jungle Book* — is very skilled in fights with rats and snakes and is not even afraid of a cobra. It can evade the snake's thrusts for as long as 45 minutes and, when the snake is exhausted, it quickly breaks its neck. However, it is not immune to snake poison. It is highly respected in India.

The **Spotted Hyena** is the 'health police' of tropical Africa; it feeds on carcasses and wastes. In the savanna it hunts antelope in family packs, considering the freshly born young the greatest delicacy. When hungry, it even attacks domestic animals.

The **Wolf** is a swift, shy and exceedingly mistrustful beast. It can recognize a trap from afar. In the winter, several families form a pack for survival. When hunting, wolves alternate as leader of the pack. No animal can outstrip their relentless run. Sometimes, part of the pack hides as an ambush and the rest drives the prey near. The young stay with their parents for two years. The wolf is the ancestor of our pet dogs. At present it lives in a large parts of Southern Europe, Asia and North America.

The **Red Fox** prefers overgrown hillsides and rocks with plenty of holes. It gives birth to up to eight young, which cannot see for 14 days. Nevertheless, they grow fast and their parents can hardly keep up with feeding them. While feeding their cubs, foxes find the courage to sneak into hen-houses and do a lot of damage. Otherwise, they mainly catch mice and other small vertebrates. They will even eat raspberries. Foxes can suffer from rabies and can infect other animals and people.

The **Raccoon Dog** lives in pairs in big forests and shore copses in the Far East. It is omnivorous, but prefers to search for dead fish. It is one of the few carnivores which hibernates, that is, sleeps during the winter.

The **Pine Marten** has a round, yellow chest and hair on the soles of its feet, so that it does not slip while climbing smooth branches. It sleeps in its hiding place during the day and only searches for food at night. Squirrels are its usual prey, but it also likes insects, eggs and sweet fruit.

The **Stone Marten** usually has a forked white chest and bare soles to its feet. It often moves into sheds and the lofts of people's houses. It also lives in towns and feeds mainly on mice and rats.

The **Common Weasel** is so slim that it can squeeze into mouse and vole holes. Its economic importance is therefore so major that it deserves full protection, although, occasionally, it attacks a bigger animal. It sometimes has white fur during the winter.

The **Stoat**, slightly bigger than the weasel, usually has white fur during the winter. Only the end of its tail remains black. It hunts mice, voles, birds and sometimes even chases small hares.

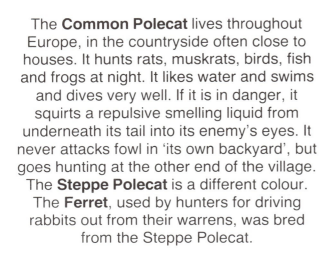

The **Common Polecat** lives throughout Europe, in the countryside often close to houses. It hunts rats, muskrats, birds, fish and frogs at night. It likes water and swims and dives very well. If it is in danger, it squirts a repulsive smelling liquid from underneath its tail into its enemy's eyes. It never attacks fowl in 'its own backyard', but goes hunting at the other end of the village. The **Steppe Polecat** is a different colour. The **Ferret**, used by hunters for driving rabbits out from their warrens, was bred from the Steppe Polecat.

The **Wolverine** moves through a deep snow by a series of arched jumps. It is very strong. It attacks animals and birds, often bigger than itself. Arrogant and cunning, it breaks into houses and evades traps. The female gives birth to two to four blind young.

The **European Badger** digs mazes of deep, long passages and keeps its set perfectly clean. It forms permanent pairs, but they live apart. It feeds on flesh and plant food.

The **European Otter** hunts fish and other water animals. It is an excellent swimmer. It is an endangered species all over Europe.

The **American Raccoon** thoroughly washes every morsel of food in water before eating it. It is an omnivore, but prefers flesh. It can create a lot of damage in hen-houses. North American farmers hunt it as often as they can. Raccoons hibernate in winter.

The **European Brown Bear** inhabits inaccessible, rocky forests. It feeds mostly at night. In December and January, two to three young are born. They are very small and the female keeps them warm during the winter. When she accompanies them through the forest in spring, she is protective and dangerous not only to other animals, but also to people.

The **Polar Bear** lives around the North Pole. Its white fur allows it to prowl unobserved in the bare ice fields. It hunts seals, whose young are its easiest prey. The female with her newborn young sleeps through the cruel winter months in a warm ice cave. The Polar Bear is a world-wide protected species.

PINNIPEDS

These aquatic mammals have streamlined bodies and their limbs form perfect oars. They have big eyes. They can dive up to 500 metres deep, can see very well under water. Some can stay under water for as long as half an hour.

The **Californian Sea Lion** lives along the shore of California. In the mating season, the males go to a common meeting place, where they fight for territory and females. The strongest male wins the most females. Throughout the entire mating season, sea lions eat no food.

The **Harbour Seal** inhabits the seas and lakes of Northern Europe. On land, it moves by bending and stretching, but in water it is very skilled and no fish can escape it. It sleeps in water, in a vertical position. During sleep, it pops up to the surface to breathe. It usually has one pup, which takes three years to become adult.

The **Walrus** lives in the polar seas. The young is suckled for about two years. It is an endangered species.

CETACEANS

The whale family includes the largest mammals in existence. They spend their entire lives in water. Whales have spindle-shaped bodies and the hind limbs are absent. The main organ of motion is a well-developed tail with a strong fin. A layer of fat, as thick as 50 cm protects them against cold. Since ancient times whales have been hunted for this fat, called blubber. Some species have already become extinct. Cetaceans are mammals and have lungs, they must surface frequently. Expired air creates clouds of steam, the shape of which helps us to identify the species.

TOOTHED WHALES

The **Sperm Whale** is one of the biggest whales and is, therefore, heavily hunted. It feeds mostly on cephalopods — tentacled creatures, such as squid and cuttlefish. It prefers warm seas, but sometimes travels far to the north.

The **Common Dolphin** lives in shoals in all seas except around the poles. It does not dive very deep and catches its main food — fish — at surface level. There are many accounts of how dolphins have saved people's lives or led ships lost in the fog safely to harbour. Many countries ban hunting dolphins.

43

WHALEBONE WHALES

The **Blue Whale** is found in all seas. The female grows up to 30 metres long; the male is a little smaller. This species is nearly extinct.

The **Greenland Whale** is a dying species of northern seas and is strictly protected. Its whalebones are some 3.5 metres long.

PROBOSCIDEANS

This type of mammal has an extended nose fused with the upper lip, into the so-called proboscis with which it conveys food and water to its mouth. In the case of elephants, this is better known as a trunk. They pluck branches, dig roots and bulbs with their tusks and peel the bark of trees. Females have teats between their front legs. Once in four years, they give birth to a single calf and suckle it for six months.

The **African Elephant** lives only in national parks and remote desert. Three thousand years ago, it was trained and used in warfare.

The **Indian Elephant** is smaller than its African cousin. Its tusks are small and sometimes they are entirely absent, but its trunk is longer. It learns well and, when domesticated, it is an excellent helper in hard work. Wild elephants living free are strictly protected.

PERISSODACTYLS

These are mostly excellent runners. Their third toe is well-developed, the others are usually rudimentary.

Mountain Zebra

Grevy's Zebra

Grant's Zebra

Innumerable herds of zebras inhabited the whole of southern and eastern Africa a long time ago. Some species became completely extinct, the remainders of others are surviving in national parks.

The **African Wild Ass** has a distinct black cross on its grey-yellow back. It is scattered in a few herds in Sahara. It is content with dry grass, but must have clean water. It was kept as a domestic animal in ancient Egypt. The **Domestic Ass** or **Donkey** is the result of many years' breeding.

The **Przewalski's Horse** is the ancestor of the Mongolian breeds of domestic horses. As a genuine wild horse, it has a short erect mane and the hair in its tail grows in two stripes. There are just a few small herds surviving in north-west China. Far more of them are kept in zoos. A lot of them can be seen also in the zoo in Prague (Czech Republic).

The **Malayan Tapir**, which lives in south-east Asia, loves forests and water. It swims well and can dive. It is shy and wary. During the day, it stays in copses; at night it grazes the leaves of bushes and trees. The young are striped.

The **Indian Rhinoceros** looks as though it is wearing armour, because its skin forms several folds on its body. Its horn does not grow from the skull, but originated from its hairs. People used to believe that this horn had magic power; as a result, the Rhinoceros was hunted so much that now it is very rarely found in the wild.

ARTIODACTYLS

These mammals stand on two toes — the third and fourth. The other toes are reduced or absent altogether. They live in herds and feed mainly on plants. The young are born highly developed; they can run a few hours after birth. They often have protective colouring. They can be found everywhere, except Australia.

NON-RUMINANTS

These animals have enlarged, upturned canines, which, when broken, continue growing.

♀   ♂

The **Wild Boar** is an omnivore, eating everything that can be eaten — roots, bulbs, fish, carcasses, berries, insects and mice. It has a great reproductive ability. It is not afraid of water and is even a good swimmer, but most of all it prefers muddy puddles, where it lies down to cool off. It roams from one place to another; at night it may travel up to 60 km. Because boars often devastated fields, they were hunted from the very beginning. In many European countries, they were exterminated. In the second half of the 20th century their numbers are slowly increasing. They avoid humans and when the female is raising piglets, she can be dangerous.

The **Hippopotamus** has completely bare nasal orifices and ears that can be closed. Its nostrils and eyes are set at the top of the head, so it can submerge its whole body and still breathe and see. There is a swimming membrane between its toes. Nowadays it lives only in national parks and inaccessible moorlands in Africa.

RUMINANTS

The stomach of these mammals comprises several different compartments. Partly digested food is regurgitated by the stomach and after a second chewing, it is digested. Bacteria and other microscopic creatures living in the stomach and gut help digestion. This enables the animal to make full use of hard, indigestible food.

The **Bactrian Camel**, the two-humped one, moves both legs on the same side, so it rocks when walking. It lives wild only on the Mongolian border. In the Asian mountains, it has been kept as a domestic animal since time immemorial because it can survive cold winters and carry heavy loads of up to 200 kg. It is content with dry, hard desert plants. Its humps do not contain water as people sometimes think.

The short-haired **Dromedary**, the one-humped one, can survive in the heat of the desert without water for several days. A number of strong breeds were bred for carrying loads and other, long-legged breeds for riding. Even the best Arab horse cannot catch up with a running camel.

The **Guanaco** lives in inaccessible places in the Cordillera Mountains in South America. A domestic form was bred from it — the **Llama**. This small humpless 'camel' can carry a load of some 50 kg.

The **Vicuña** is a little smaller. It has extremely soft hair; the most valuable tuft of longer wool is on its breast. The Incas used to spin this wool to make the softest and most expensive cloth for their rulers and their retinue. International effort has succeeded in rescuing the Vicuña from extinction.

The **Alpaca**, with its very long hair, is a descendant of the Guanaco.

The **Red Deer** is found all over Europe and has many subspecies. It was driven from the borders to the depth of the forests. In February, the male sheds his antlers; by August he has grown new ones, usually with one more point. It lives in herds, males separately from the females and young. The rutting season starts in the first half of September. The following May, the female gives birth to one young and suckles it until winter.

The **Fallow Deer**, smaller than the Red Deer, is kept in deer parks as well as roaming wild. It likes bright groves and glades.

The **Roe Deer**, the most widespread hoofed game, prefers forest borders verging on meadows and fields. The rutting season lasts from June to August. In May, the females usually give birth to two young, which can run when ten days old.

The **European Moose** lives in moorlands and sparse forests. It feeds on water plants and leaves; its favourite food is the bitter bark of trees. It had become extinct in Western and Central Europe by the 14th century; some specimens can be still found in Poland and Russia.

The **Reindeer** is an exception among deer — both females and males have antlers. In winter, individual groups get together in herds of thousands and move in search of food, led by a mature experienced female. The semi-domesticated reindeer pulls sledges and provides fatty milk, meat and warm fur.

The **Giraffe** lives in the African steppe where there is a sparse growth of acacia and feeds on its leaves. When it wants to drink, it has to spread its front legs so that it can reach down to the water. It lives in small groups. It is an ambler, but when it runs, it jumps with both its front legs and then its hind legs together. It is the only mammal which does not make any sound.

The **European Bison**, which once lived in Europe's forests, survives only in the Polish national park of Bielowe. At present, it is kept in reserves.

The **American Bison** is the animal of endless prairies. Millions of bison were ruthlessly slaughtered by white immigrants. Now only a few herds live in national parks.

The **Water Buffalo** or **Arnee** always stays close to water, in which it can lie the whole day. It is often cross-bred with the domesticated buffalo, which is its descendant. Apart from the elephant, the wild buffalo is the only animal in the jungle which is not afraid of tigers.

White-tailed Gnu

Lesser Kudu

Springbok

Gemsbok

The antelopes form a large group of fast animals, living mainly in the African steppe. The individual specimens differ from each other very much.

The **Chamois** is at home in the high mountains of Europe. It lives in small groups in high meadows above the tree line. In unfavourable conditions, it can survive on buds, bark, and moss. Its worst enemy is a hard winter.

The **Musk-ox** lives on the north shore of Canada and in Greenland. It is also found in the Siberian Arctic. It wanders in small herds; only very old bulls lead a lonely life.

The **Ibex** climbs even higher than the Chamois and leaves the mountain heights only during very cold winters. It was hunted for its beautiful horns and delicious meat and nearly became extinct, but now the numbers are slowly increasing again.

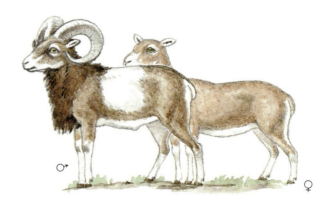

The **Wild Goat** is on the brink of extinction. The remainders of its herds have been preserved in Asia Minor and the Mediterranean. Occasionally, it is bred in reserves in Central Europe, where it reproduces well. It is the ancestor of the Domestic Goat.

The **Mouflon**, which lives wild only in Sardinia and Corsica, was imported to other parts of Europe as game. It thrives best in Bohemia and Slovakia. This mountain sheep lives in small herds, usually led by a mature experienced female.

HOW MAMMALS LIVE

The Deer is happy in a quiet corner protected from the wind.

The Hare has a shallow form in fields. In its territory it makes more burrows.

The Lesser Horseshoe Bat sleeps all day in hollow trees, caves, old galleries and house lofts.

The Harvest Mouse builds a small round nest of grass, about 50 cm above the ground, in a tangle of reed or corn stalks.

The Squirrel makes a round nest from branches and grass, lined with moss and hay, in the trees. As well as this, it has a few other hiding places, often rebuilt abandoned nests of birds of prey.

The Hamster has a complete underground residence — a vertical entrance, a slanting exit, a softly lined bedroom, a big pantry and even a toilet.

The Otter digs its burrow in steep, overgrown riverbanks. One entrance is below water level, the other on the land among stones or roots. Its den is always above water level.

The Muskrat also burrows passages in the banks or builds a big heap from branches and reeds, which sometimes floats. It is called a lodge. Entrances and exits are below water level, but the bedrooms are always dry.

The Bear lives in a cave or digs a lair under a large fallen tree.

The Fox digs a big underground maze with several exits, preferably under tree roots in stony ground. It has several other dens for various occasions in its hunting territory.

THE YOUNG OF MAMMALS

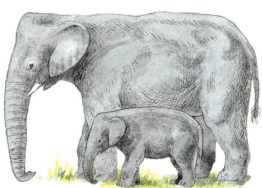

The Elephant gives birth to one calf once every three or four years.

The Whale usually has one young every two years.

The Horse produces one foal a year.

The Cat has up to eight kittens in one year.

The Hare produces up to four litters of six young a year.

The Common Vole is extremely fertile — it can have up to 18 in one litter even six times a year!

WHAT THEY LOOK LIKE WHEN THEY ARE BORN

The Rabbit produces its litter in a warm, dark den. The kits are blind and completely bare.

The Hedgehog's young are also blind and bare. Soft spines start to grow after a few hours.

The Bat is born with fur. It sucks milk from its mother's teat and holds tight to her fur to avoid falling during flight.

The Hare's young have fur and can see immediately. They are born in the open, even on snow. With their greybrown fur, they merge with the earth of the fields in which they live.

The Roe Deer's young have white spots. In a glade they practically disappear among blooming flowers. They can stand up on their own soon after being born.

The Monkey can see when born, has hair and can move quite soon afterwards. It develops more quickly than human children.

WHAT ANTLERS ARE

Horns, which are of horny substance covering bony holders, last the animal its whole life, but antlers are bony and are exchanged every year. They grow from protrusions of frontal bone, so called 'burrs', at the age of 12 months. To begin with, they are soft and protected with sensitive hairy skin, the 'velvet'. When the antlers mature, the velvet dries and peels off. The animal gets rid of it by rubbing its antlers against the trunks of young trees and finally eats it.

The young deer develops its first antlers in the second year of its life, usually in September, and sheds them next May. The second antlers begin growing immediately and the velvet is rubbed off in August. These antlers are forked. Every year the antlers get bigger and have more 'branches'. Huntsmen count the 'branches' on both antlers. A six-tined, or branched, stag is a deer which has three tines on each antler. In old age the antlers get thinner and have fewer tines.

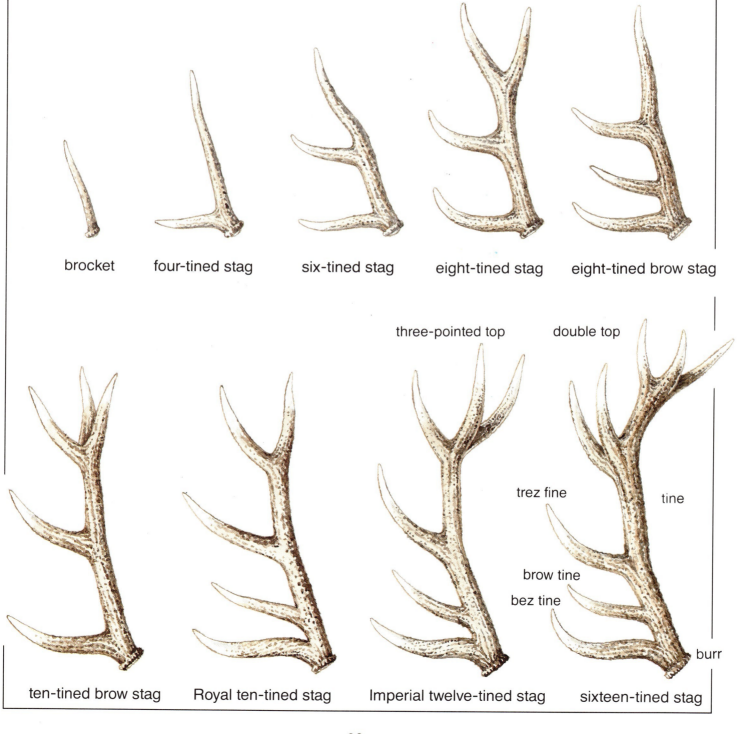

brocket   four-tined stag   six-tined stag   eight-tined stag   eight-tined brow stag

three-pointed top   double top

trez fine   tine

brow tine

bez tine

burr

ten-tined brow stag   Royal ten-tined stag   Imperial twelve-tined stag   sixteen-tined stag

WHY SOME MAMMALS HAVE A LARGE BODY SURFACE

The Indian Elephant, living in shadowy jungle, has relatively small ears.

The African Elephant lives in a hot climate. To prevent its body overheating, it needs as large a body surface as possible. Therefore, it has huge ears.

The European Hare and the Red Fox live in a moderate climate. They have quite long ears and legs.

The Arctic Hare and the Arctic Fox must preserve as much bodily warmth as possible in the cold north. Therefore, although they are quite big, they have short legs, tails and ears to make the body surface as small as possible and thermal regulation easier.

GENUINE AND FALSE WINTER SLEEPERS

Some animals would not be able to find enough food during the winter, so they pass this season in a state of suspension, called hibernation. Their body temperature drops and their heart beats more slowly. During this sleep, they do not eat. They wake up with the arrival of warm spring days. We call them genuine sleepers.

The Hedgehog makes a den in a pile of leaves or under some wood and rolls up into a ball. If the frost is very heavy, it wakes up and burrows deeper.

The European Badger, which is very broad and fat, closes all entrances to its castle before winter.

The Alpine Marmot digs a den up to 3 metres deep in the earth. It usually sleeps there, with the whole family, for seven months because mountain winter comes early and spring comes late.

The European Suslik sleeps through the winter in about 1 metre deep underground.

Bats collect in their habitual wintering places in caves and abandoned mines. They need absolute peace and a constant temperature of about 6 °C.

The Dormouse makes its den in a hollow tree or under tree roots, lines it with hay and covers itself with its thick tail. It sleeps for six months.

The mammals, which wake up during the winter and eat some food from time to time, are called false sleepers. Their body temperature does not drop during their sleep.

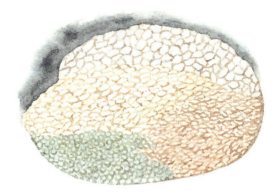

The Hamster is well prepared for the winter. It collects and stores up to 15 kg of corn, turnip, peas and potatoes.

The Bear does not sleep much — only a few weeks altogether — and gets up from time to time to take an airing. Only the female with her young spends longer in the den. The Bear does not mind being snowed in and does not gather any reserves. It lives on its fat.

WHOSE TRAIL IS IT?

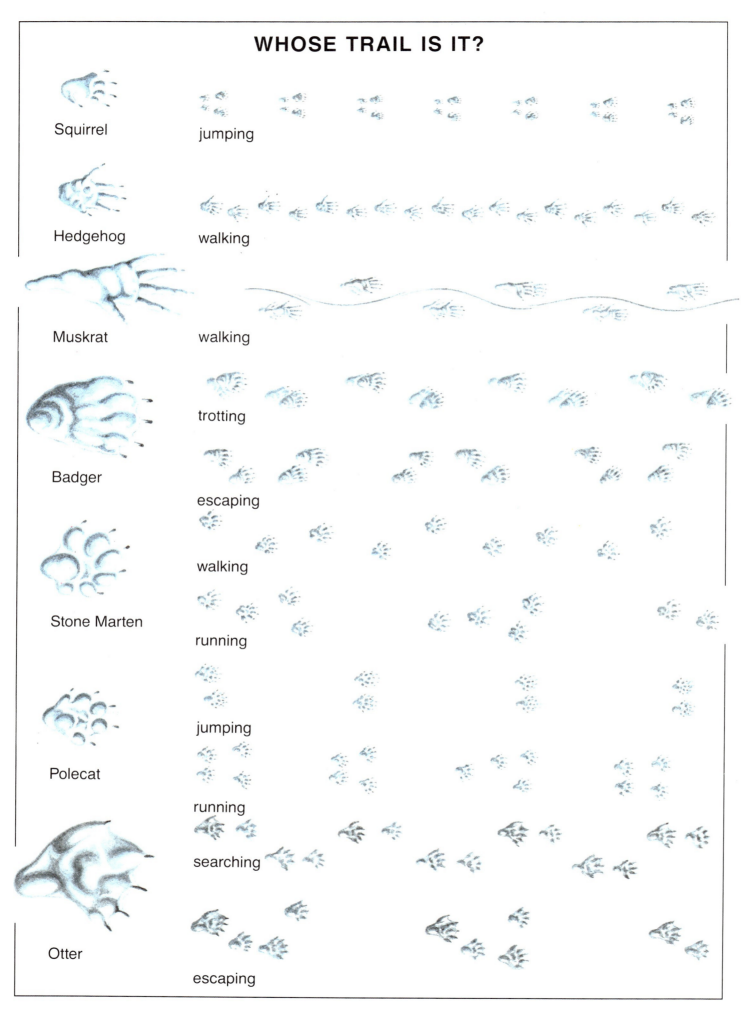

Squirrel   jumping

Hedgehog   walking

Muskrat   walking

Badger   trotting

         escaping

Stone Marten   walking

         running

         jumping

Polecat   running

         searching

Otter   escaping

64

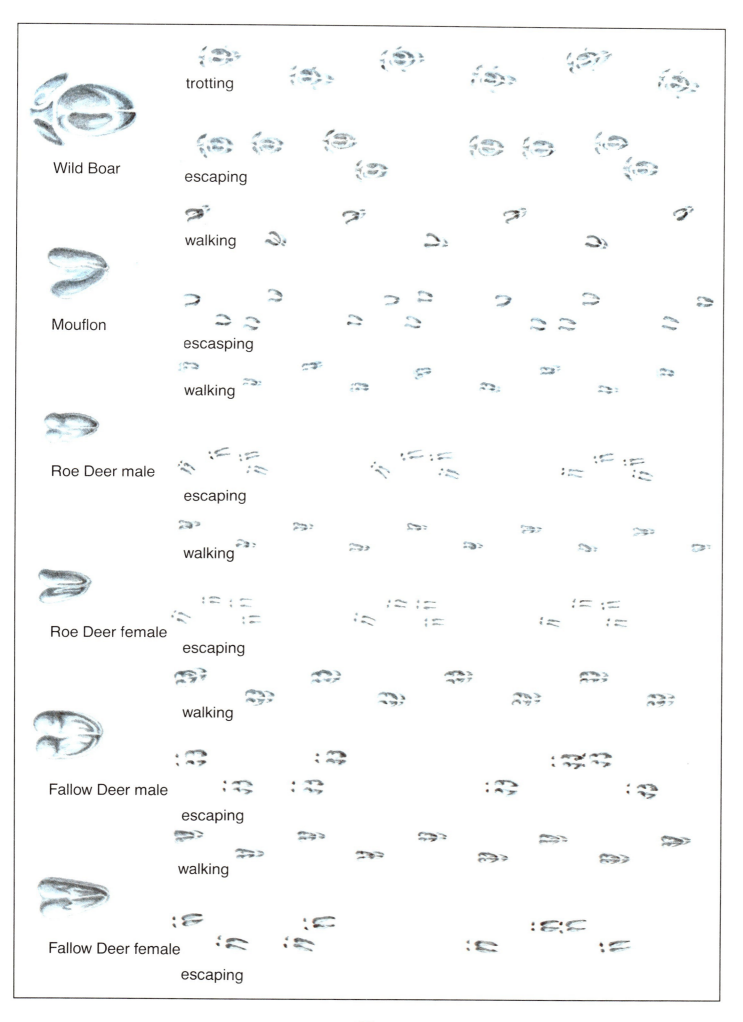

Wild Boar

trotting

escaping

Mouflon

walking

escasping

Roe Deer male

walking

escaping

Roe Deer female

walking

escaping

Fallow Deer male

walking

escaping

Fallow Deer female

walking

escaping

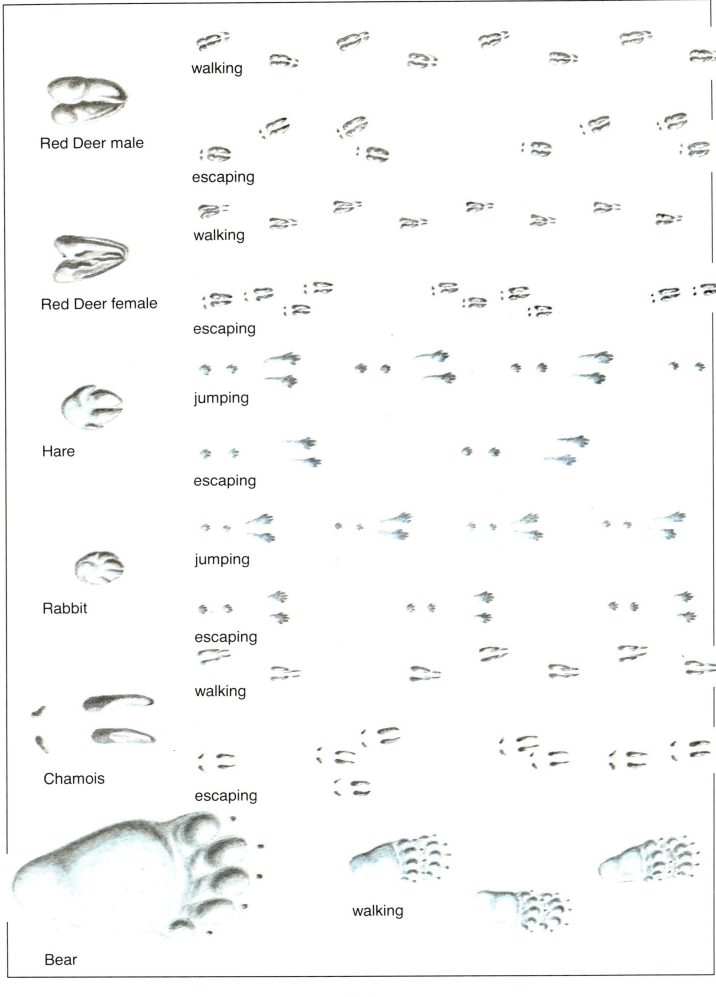

Red Deer male

walking

escaping

Red Deer female

walking

escaping

Hare

jumping

escaping

Rabbit

jumping

escaping

walking

Chamois

escaping

Bear

walking

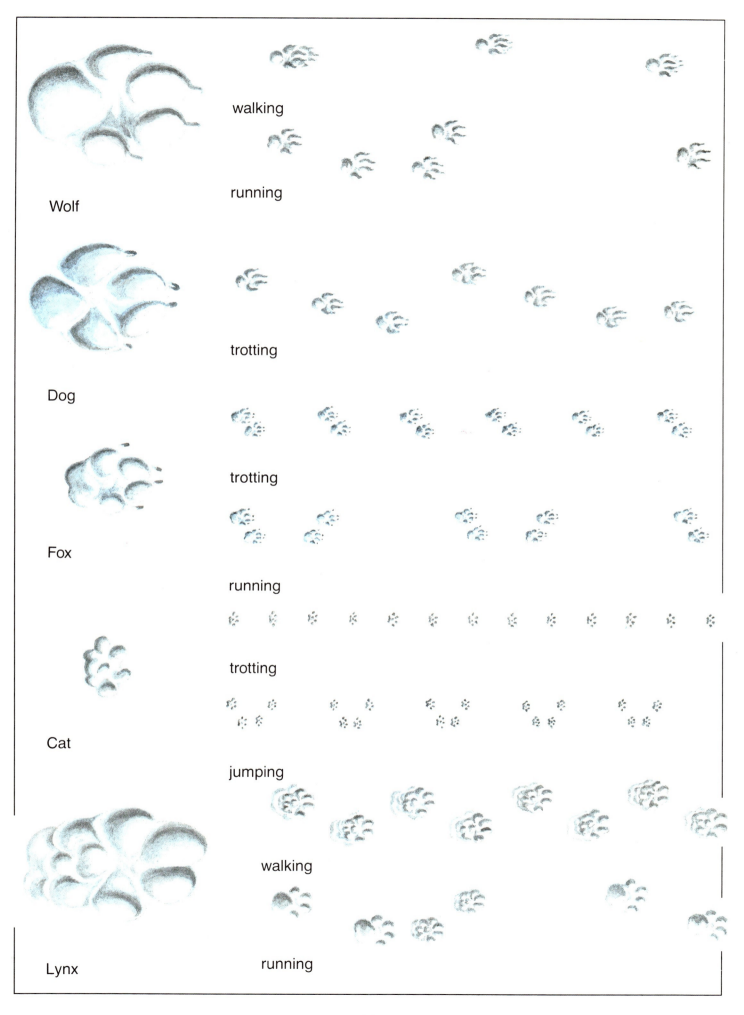

Wolf

walking

running

Dog

trotting

Fox

trotting

running

Cat

trotting

jumping

Lynx

walking

running

WHERE MAMMALS LIVE

A long time ago, the land mass of the Earth was all in one piece. In the course of millions of years, it split up and its parts became more and more distant. The animals living in these parts began to develop differently. For this reason the animals of all continents are different. Scientists divided the whole world into six main zoogeographic regions.

Neo-Arctic region

Neo-Tropical region

Palaeo-Arctic region

Ethiopian region

Indo-Malaysian region

Australian region

Mountain Lion

Harbour Seal

Walrus

American Bison

American Raccoon

Californian Sea Lion

Musk-ox

Wapiti Deer

Wolf

Polar Bear

European Moose

Jaguar

Brown Capuchin

Two-toed Sloth

Wild Guinea Pig

Anteater

Brazilian Tapir

Armadillo

Guanaco

Fennec

Ibex

Chamois

European Bison

Red Deer

Wild Boar

Common Dolphin

Greenland Whale

Sperm Whale

Przewalski's Horse

Lynx

European Brown Bear

Reindeer

Siberian Tiger

Bactrian Camel

Giraffe

Springbok

Mantled Baboon

African Elephant

Lion

Spotted Hyena

Hippopotamus

Chimpanzee

Black Rhinoceros

Cheetah

White-tailed Gnu

Ring-tailed Lemur

Indian Elephant

Indian Rhinoceros

Indian Tiger

Orang-utan

Malayan Fruit Bat

Platypus

Koala

Australian Echidna

Grey Kangaroo

MAMMALS OF DAY AND MAMALS OF NIGHT

Chimpanzee

Anteater

Red Squirrel

Alpine Marmot

Arctic Fox

Cheetah

Honey Badger

Klipspringer

Philippine Tarsier

Two-toed Sloth

Fat Dormouse

Common Porcupine

Fennec

Jungle Cat

European Badger

Grey Duiker

70

WHICH MAMMALS WERE IMPORTED TO EUROPE?

The Muskrat comes from North America. At the beginning of the 20th century it was brought to Dobříš in Bohemia.

The Mouflon, the mountain sheep of Sardinia and Corsica, appeared in Europe in the 19th century.

The Fallow Deer comes from the Mediterranean and Asia Minor. It has been bred in deer parks since the end of the Middle Ages.

The Sika Deer, a beautiful small deer of Japanese and Chinese origin, is also often kept in parks.

The Wild Goat from Asia Minor can be found in many parts of Central Europe.

The White-tailed Deer was brought to Europe from North America.

The Wild Rabbit, originally from Spain, was already widespread in the 13th century.

DOMESTIC MAMMALS

People have been domesticating some mammals since time immemorial, trying to use them for their own needs. By careful selection and breeding, people achieved the result they sought. After thousands of years, different breeds of horses, cattle, pigs, sheep, goats, rabbits, cats and dogs were developed.

Boxer

St. Bernard

Bedlington Terrier

Pekinese

Czech Wirehaired Pointer

Wire-haired Dachshund

English Cocker Spaniel

Great Dane — Harlequin

Bull Terrier

Basset Hound

Wire Fox Terrier

Miniature Pinscher

Chow-chow

German Spitz

Borzoi

Collie

German Shepherd Dog

Shetland Pony

Arabian Horse

Belgian Horse

Kladruby Horse

Hucul Horse

Czech Red-spotted Cattle

Jersey Cattle

Danish Red Cattle

Friesian Cattle

Hampshire Pig

White bred Pig

Vietnam Pig

Cornwall Pig

Merino Sheep

Caracul Sheep

Suffolk Sheep

Somalian Sheep

Sanian Goat

Harz Goat

Belgian Giant Rabbit

Czech Spotted Rabbit

French Ram Rabbit

Angora Rabbit

European Three-coloured Cat

Persian Cat

Siamese Cat

MAMMALS IN THE LABORATORY

Some mammals are kept as experimental animals. They are used, for example, for experiments with new medicaments, which are introduced to the market according to the results of these tests.

White Mouse

Black Mouse

White Rat

Guinea Pig

Golden Hamster

Rabbit

Horak's laboratory dog

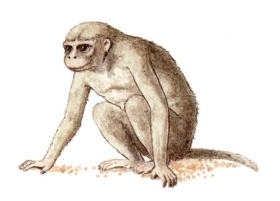

Rhesus Monkey

WHICH SPECIES OF MAMMALS ARE ENDANGERED?

Shrews

White-toothed Shrews

Bats

Economic Vole

Horseshoe Bats

Hedgehogs

Wild Dormouse

Common Dormouse

Snow Vole

Garden Dormouse

Northern Birch Mouse

Alpine Marmot

European Brown Bear

Chamois

European Otter

Mediterranean Monk Seal

Harp Seal

European Moose

INDEX

Numbers in bold refer to main entries.